Haymeadows near Thwaite in Swaledale. The meadows of the Dales, especially along Wensleydale and Swaledale, are some of the last remaining areas of unimproved flower-rich northern pasture. Typical species include meadow buttercup, common sorrel, crane's-bill, pignut, red fescue, Yorkshire fog and lady's mantle. The fields are ungrazed from June until ready to cut in July and August. The grass is left to dry before being baled. The many fieldbarns were used to store the hay close to the stock for winter feeding.

Yorkshire Pudding

120g/4oz plain flour, 1 egg (beaten), 150ml/¼ pt milk, 150ml/¼ pt water, pinch salt.

Sieve the flour and salt into a bowl, and make a well in the centre. Drop in the egg and start beating with a whisk, bringing in the flour gradually. As the batter thickens, add the milk and water in stages bringing in more flour gradually all the time. Leave to stand for at least 30 minutes then give a final beating before cooking.

Put 30g/1oz lard or dripping (or oil) in a 25x30 cm (10"x12") baking tin, or put a little fat in each of the sections (about 15) of muffin tins. Place in an oven, preheated to 220°C/425°F/gas mark 7. When the fat is smoking hot, pour in batter quickly and carefully. Cook for 20 minutes, or until risen and browned.

Yorkshire pudding was originally cooked underneath the meat while it spit roasted by the fire. A pan with some dripping was placed on the fire and the batter poured in when it was smoking hot. A high heat is needed to get a light pudding. As the meat cooked, the juices dripped into the pudding.

When domestic ovens were introduced during the 19th century, Yorkshire Pudding was moved above the meat, as the hottest part of the oven is at the top. Yorkshire Pudding is traditionally eaten with gravy first, with the main course of meat and vegetables following.

The Yorkshire Dales: Limestone and Falls

Many of the distinctive natural features of the western Dales are due to the underlying limestone, which has flat bedding planes and vertical joints running through it. The rivers flow along the flat bedding planes, but every so often erode along the line of a vertical joint, dropping in falls and rapids.

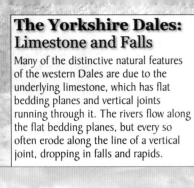

Above: Wain Wath Falls at the west end of Swaledale. Top right: Thornton Force on the Ingleton Waterfalls Trail. The words 'force' and 'foss' were brought by Viking settlers. Bottom right: Aysgarth Falls on the River Ure in Wensleydale.

Above: Malham Cove was formed as the land moved on either side of the Craven Fault. Below: The view across the limestone pavement on the top of Malham Cove. In the nearest fields on the right hand side ridges can be seen, the result of Saxon and Medieval ploughing and Iron Age and Romano-British walls.

Pennine Oatcakes

Without a bakstone or practice at throwing the mixture, it is not possible to make soft oatcakes in the traditional way. This is a simpler recipe written down in the 1940s in the Nelson and Colne area about 12 miles from Skipton, just over the Lancashire border.

2 tbs/50g plain flour, 1 tbs/30g fine oatmeal, 8 fl oz/225ml half and half milk and water, pinch of salt.

Put the flour and oatmeal in a bowl, and gradually whisk in the liquid to make a smooth mixture about the consistency of pancake batter. It can be left to stand and whisked again to make it smoother, but it will thicken so add a little more liquid.

Pour about a quarter of the mixture in the centre of hot, well greased pan and swirl round so the mixture is in a thin round disc. Cook for a couple of minutes until all of the top of the oatcake looks cooked, by which time the bottom should be a good brown colour. Flip over and cook the other side until browned.

Serve with bacon, black pudding, eggs or grated cheese.

Below: Skipton in the southern Dales, where soft oatcakes were made. John Leech of Skipton supplied Simpson's-in-the-Strand and London Clubs with oatcakes for many years.

In 1782, the 33rd Regiment of Foot became The 1st Yorkshire West Riding Regiment, in recognition of the area where it recruited. The regiment was already known unofficially as 'The Havercake Lads'.

The Yorkshire Dales: Oatcakes, north and south

Oatcakes are the traditional 'bread' of Yorkshire. Oats grew well through much of Yorkshire and most farmers grew for their own consumption and to sell locally. Wheat had to be bought for cash, so wheatflour was reserved for special occasions.

There were two types of oatcake. The first was a hard kind of oatcake, similar to the Scottish oatcakes produced today. These were made in the northern part of the Yorkshire Dales and into Westmorland and Cumberland. It was also known as 'clap bread', from the noise that was made as the firm mixture of oatmeal and water was slapped by the hand into a thin cake, having been placed on a board. This was famously described in 1698 by Celia Fiennes in 'Through England on a Side Saddle in the Time of William and Mary'.

The other type was a softer, thinner oatcake several inches across. These were made in the North York Moors, the south and west of Yorkshire and over the Pennines into East Lancashire. These were made with a mixture of oatmeal, water and either yeast or sourdough, which was left to ferment overnight. Sourdough was a portion of the previous batch of mixture which was kept and was still fermenting. In a remote farmhouse this avoided having to obtain fresh yeast and it also added to the flavour.

The commonest description of the technique was that a ladleful of mixture was put onto a meal covered cloth, and then thrown onto a hot bakstone. The bakstone was usually a piece of slate heated over a firebox. A skilled throw would spread the oatcake mixture very thinly, and so it did not need turning over to cook the other side. The small holes that formed in the surface gave them these oatcakes their other name - riddle bread. They were either eaten fresh and soft, or hung up on a rack near the ceiling to dry so they could be stored for eating later.

Below: Thwaite in Swaledale; an area where hard oatcakes were preferred.

The Yorkshire Dales:
The Three Peaks

From left to right: Pen-y-ghent (694m), Whernside (736m) and Ingleborough (723m). Rising around the head of the River Ribble they are mostly limestone like the surrounding areas, with many underground cave systems. However, these mountains have a cap of hard Millstone Grit, which resisted the ice age glaciers as they ground down the surrounding landscape.

On top of Ingleborough (right) was the highest altitude Iron Age hill-fort in Britain, in use before the Roman occupation. A stone wall enclosed twenty circular stone buildings which were occupied during the summer while the high pastures were being grazed.

What is a 'cake'?

Over the last 50 years, descriptions have become more specific; cakes are light and sweet, brownies dense, biscuits crisp, cookies crumbly and pastries are named after their crust. But in the past a 'cake' could be any of those items. They could also be plain bread 'buns', such as a Yorkshire teacakes or Lancashire barmcakes, or the oatcakes described earlier. They could even contain meat; in the north Pennines, tatie cake was a traybake with a meat and potato filling between two layers of pastry.

'Sad' Cakes

Some cakes usually sink in the centre after baking, and these are called 'sad' cakes. Parkin and gingerbread are often baked this way. The centre is very moist and quite dense in contrast to the lighter texture near the edge and the sticky top and sides - almost like three cakes in one!

Pastry type cakes would never rise much at all were also described as 'sad'.

The Settle-Carlisle line was built through the Dales by the Midland Railway as their route to Scotland. It was an engineering challenge, with fourteen tunnels and more than twenty viaducts, including the famous one at Ribblehead. Below, 30777 'Sir Lamiel' runs north over the Dent Head viaduct.

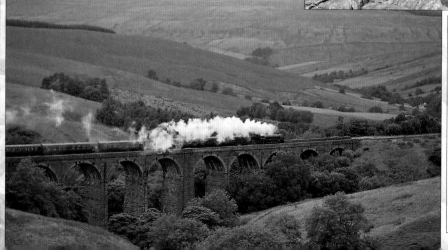

Limestone Pavement, as seen above and on Malham Cove on an earlier page, is a special feature of the Dales. Rainwater on the flat surface of the limestone finds and erodes along the vertical joint lines, creating gaps (grykes) and leaving blocks (clints). The sheltered grykes create a suitable environment for lime-loving plants, including many types of ferns, as well as wall lettuce, biting stonecrop, rue-leaved saxifrage, blue moor-grass, wild thyme, limestone bedstraw, common rock-rose, geranium, wood anemone and enchanter's nightshade.

Yorkshire Spice Loaf

[35]0g/12oz strong flour, 125g/4oz butter, 1 beaten egg, 90g/3oz caster sugar, 250g/9oz [cu]rrants or other dried fruit, 25g/1oz mixed peel, 2 tsp traditional dried yeast, [20]0ml/7floz milk, 1 tsp mixed spice, ½ tsp each of cinnamon, nutmeg and salt.

[W]arm the milk to blood heat - very warm but not too hot to hold your finger in it - [t]hen whisk in the yeast and 1 tsp sugar, then leave in a warm place for 15 minutes or [u]ntil bubbling well. Meanwhile, sift together flour, spices and [s]alt, then rub in the butter. Stir in the remaining sugar and [d]ried fruit. Beat the egg into yeast mixture and stir it into the [fl]our mixture with a wooden spoon, to make a soft dough. [P]ut in a greased and lined 22x11x6 cm/2 lb loaf tin and leave [i]n a warm place* for an hour or more to rise. It is ready to [b]ake when it rises above the top of the tin. Bake for 1 hour at [1]50°C/300°F/gas mark 2, or until cooked in the centre.

[*Between 20°C and 30°C is ideal. Avoid direct heat; in an airing [c]upboard is better than by a fire or radiator. Too much heat [w]ill kill the yeast, and too little heat will slow down the rise.

Fruit loaves are the simplest of cakes for special occasions. Originally, some dried fruit was added to an ordinary dough mix, maybe along with some extra fat. They became sweeter as sugar became cheaper during the early 18th century, and an egg would also make it richer and crumblier. Most cake recipes started to use chemical raising agents after Alfred Bird invented a fast and easy modern form of baking powder in 1843, but in Yorkshire, spice loaf continued to be made with yeast.

Below left: Burnsall lies on the River Wharfe north of The Strid and Bolton Abbey.

Below right: Near Bolton Abbey, the River Wharfe passes through a narrow valley in a series of fast flowing waterfalls and rapids known as The Strid. On either side lies Strid Wood, which is one of the best places for ancient semi-natural sessile oak woodland in the Yorkshire Dales National Park.

Left: East Witton. Methodism was very strong in the Dales, and they built their small, modest chapels in many villages.

Left: Brimham Rocks have been a tourist attraction since the 18th century, when many of the strange shaped formations were given names. The tors are made of Millstone grit, probably carved by chemical action and differential weathering of the layers, rather than the more usual explanation of wind erosion.

Above: West Tanfield is a picturesque village on the edge of the Yorkshire Dales and the Vale of Mowbray, the stone rooves of the Dales giving way to tiles. Near the church is the Marmion Tower, a 15th century gatehouse which survived the manor house of the Marmion family. There is a fine example of an oriel window on the first floor.

The Methodists held outdoor 'Love Feasts' during the late 19th century, which included one for 1,500 people at Brimham. Scripture Cake, with its biblical references was served at these events, as well as being contributed to many church fundraising cookbooks.

4½ cupfuls of I Kings, iv, 22;
1½ cupfuls of Judges, v, 25 (last clause);
2 cupfuls of Jeremiah, vi, 20 (2nd item);
2 cupfuls of I Samuel, xxx, 12 (2nd item);
2 cupfuls Of Nahum, iii, 12;
1 cupful of Numbers, xvii, 8;
4 tbs of Judges, iv, 19 (last clause);
2 tbs of I Samuel, xiv, 25;
Season to taste of Chronicles ix, 9;
4 of Jeremiah, xvii, 11;
A pinch of Leviticus, ii, 13;
2 tsp Amos, iv, 5.
Follow Solomon's prescriptions for making a good boy - Proverbs xxiii, 14.

Scripture Cake

225g/8oz flour, 110g/4oz butter, 110g/4oz soft brown sugar, 110g/4oz raisins, 110g/4oz figs, 55g/2oz flaked/chopped almonds, 2 tbs milk, 1 tbs honey, ½ tsp mixed spice, 2 eggs, pinch salt, 1 tsp baking powder.

Beat together the butter, sugar and honey, then beat in the eggs. Add the dried fruit and nuts and beat again. Sieve together the flour, baking powder, spice and salt, then stir in, followed by the milk. Put into a greased and lined 18 cm/7" round tin and bake for 1¼ hours at 170°C/325°F/ gas mark 3.

Left: Ripon Cathedral. St Wilfred, or Wilfra, was important in early Christianity. After four years in the Celtic foundation on Lindisfarne he travelled to Rome and started promoting Roman customs and monasticism in Britain. His remains were buried in the cathedral near the High Altar.

The Feast of St. Wilfrid, was held in Ripon on the Sunday following Lammas-day, during August. The start of the feast is ancient but unknown. However it is known that horse races were first held in 1713 and long processions were held in the 19th century as part of a week of festivities.

Wilfra Tarts were made to be given away on the day of the procession. Other kinds of tarts were also made, such as jam tarts and pastries similar to the almond cheesecake recipe in this booklet.

Apple Pie without the Cheese is like a Kiss without a Squeeze

There is a strong tradition in Yorkshire of eating cheese with both apple pie and fruit cake, and this quote often crops up. While the first printed record of the quote is from the USA in the late 19th century, it was probably part of an old English rhyme from around 1750 which was taken to America by settlers.

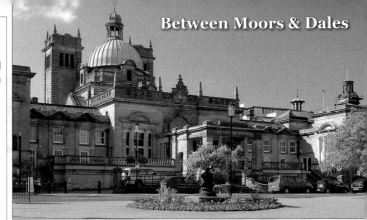

Above: Harrogate. The first mineral spring was discovered in 1571 and by 1770 Harrogate was a well established Spa. From the coming of the railway in 1840 to the start of the First World War, Harrogate was a highly fashionable health resort based on hydrotherapy. However, it ceased to be a spa in 1969 when the Royal Baths closed. During the Second World War government departments were moved to Harrogate, leading to it becoming an important exhibition and conference centre.

The Vale of Mowbray, between the Yorkshire Dales and the Hambleton Hills, has a remarkable number of Neolithic monuments. There are six large henges, three together near Thornborough, the largest number outside of Wessex. However, those remains are low-lying and best seen from the air.

More conspicuous are the three remaining standing stones of the Devil's Arrows (below left) near Boroughbridge (below right). Standing in a line, little is known about them, but legend holds that the Devil threw them from How Hill, south of Fountains Abbey, towards Aldborough but they fell short. Boroughbridge has a recorded history from Roman times. It was an important staging post on the Great North Road to Scotland, but was bypassed by the main rail line north and so it remained a small, attractive market town.

WILFRA TART

Filling: 450g/1lb cooking apple – peeled, cored and thinly sliced. 60g/2oz light soft brown sugar. ½ tbs flour. 110g/4oz grated Wensleydale cheese.
Shortcrust pastry: 150g/5oz flour. 75g/2½oz butter.

Make up the pastry as described on the inside back page. Roll out half and line a 20 cm/8" flan or pie dish. Mix the apple, flour and sugar together and put into the pastry case, then spread the cheese over the top. Roll out the remaining pastry, damp the edge of the pastry in the dish and place the lid over, sealing the edges well. Cut slits in the top, then glaze with milk or egg.

Bake at 190°C/375°F/gas mark 5 for 30 minutes.. The pastry should be browned and the juices just starting to bubble out of the slits. If the pastry is browning too quickly, just turn the oven down a little.

Across the North York Moors:
Turf Cakes and Fat Rascals

"Away on the left, but scarcely discernible, was Swart Houe Cross, on Egton Low Moor, and straight in front lay the Skelder Inn... I stepped into the little parlour, with its sanded floor, and demanded 'fat rascals' and tea. The girl was not surprised at my request, for the hot turf cakes supplied at the inn are known to all the neighbourhood by this unusual name, although they are not particularly fat, and are so extremely palatable that one would gladly call them by a friendlier name. 'Yorkshire Painted And Described' by Gordon Home, 1908.

Throughout Britain there are recipes similar to turf cakes; in Wales, Welsh cakes or pice ar y maen, in Durham and Northumberland, singin' hinnies, in East Lancashire and West Yorkshire, sad cakes and suet cakes. All were cooked on a bakstone or griddle, like a heavy frying pan, over the fire.

There was another way of cooking on an open fire, by putting bread and cakes in a lidded pot placed in the ash. It was a short step from cooking in a pot to baking in an oven, as fat rascals are cooked today.

Turf Cakes

250g/8oz self-raising flour, 45g/1½oz caster sugar, 125g/4oz butter, 60g/2oz currants, 30g/1oz sultanas.

Sieve together the flour and sugar, then rub in the butter. Stir in the dried fruit then mix and cut in the milk with a knife until the mixture comes together as a soft dough, adding a little more milk if needed. For a richer mixture use a beaten egg instead of the milk. Place the mixture on a floured surface, roll out 12mm/½" thick and cut out small rounds. Cook on a lightly greased griddle or a heavy-based frying pan (cast iron is ideal) over a low-medium heat. Each side should brown in about 3 minutes, by which time the centre should be just cooked. Eat them while they are still warm; you may like them as they are, or they can be split and buttered.

In some recipes it is cooked in one large round, but it is difficult to turn it over if using a frying pan rather than a traditional bakstone or griddle.

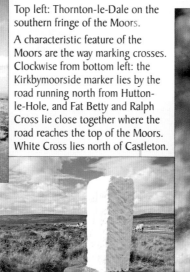

Top left: Thornton-le-Dale on the southern fringe of the Moors.

A characteristic feature of the Moors are the way marking crosses. Clockwise from bottom left: the Kirkbymoorside marker lies by the road running north from Hutton-le-Hole, and Fat Betty and Ralph Cross lie close together where the road reaches the top of the Moors. White Cross lies north of Castleton.

Fat Rascals

225g/8oz self-raising flour, 110g/4oz butter, 55g/2oz light soft brown sugar, 85g/3oz mixed currants and sultanas, milk and water to mix (about 3 tbs). 6 glacé cherries and some angelica (optional). Makes 5 or 6.

Rub the fat into the flour, then stir in the sugar and dried fruit. Mix to a soft dough with milk and water. Roll out about 1cm/½" thick and cut out 8cm/3" rounds. Decorate with half cherries and angelica and brush with milk. Bake for 15-20 minutes at 190°C/375°F/ gas mark 5 until the surface is tinged brown.

he Hole of Horcum (above) is about 125m deep and over a kilometre across. It was formed when huge amounts of water flooded from a glacial lake at the end of the last Ice Age. A local legend ells another story; it was created by a giant who scooped out a handful of earth to throw at his wife. At Sutton Bank (below) the main road climbs the steep escarpment which was carved by a lacier as it ground down the Vale of Mowbray during the last Ice Age. During the Iron Age 2,500 years ago, British tribes constructed a large and imposing hill fort at this site.

Yorkshire Parkins

170g/6oz flour, 170g/6oz medium oatmeal, 110g/4oz soft brown sugar, 110g/4oz butter, 110g/4oz black treacle or golden syrup, 2 tsp bicarb soda, 3 tsp ground ginger, 1 tsp mixed spice.

Sieve together the dry ingredients, rub in the butter, then stir in the treacle or syrup to make a dough. With floured hands, divide into about 20 pieces. Form each into a ball, place on greased baking sheets leaving room to spread, and flatten to about 9 mm/3/8" thick. Bake at 170°C/325°F/gas mark 3 for 12-15 minutes, just until they are turning colour.

Leave to cool a little before taking off the sheets. They should be crisp on the outside and chewier in the middle. Put in an air-tight tin as soon as they have cooled.

Australian Brownies

125g/5oz butter (melted), 200g/8oz granulated sugar, 100g/4oz porridge oats, 125g/5oz plain flour, 100g/4oz desiccated coconut, 1 tbs golden syrup dissolved in 2 tbs hot water, 1 tsp bicarbonate of soda.

Use the same method as for Yorkshire Parkins, except stir in the butter instead of rubbing, and divide into 20-30 pieces. Bake for 15 minutes until golden brown.

Parkins are widely known within Britain, from Cheshire to Scotland, although recipes vary. Emigrants to Australia and New Zealand would have taken recipes with them.

During the First World War, what seems like a variation of parkins was sent by families to Anzac troops fighting in Turkey, as they would keep on the long sea voyage. Certainly, by 1925 there were published recipes similar to this one. They are still made to raise funds for war veteran's organisations around Anzac Day.

James Cook was brought up in Great Ayton. There is now a museum in the schoolroom, with a statue nearby (left).

He was apprenticed in a grocer's shop in Staithes (above), but left and went to Whitby (right) to become a seaman. Rising through the ranks to Captain, his main three voyages of discovery on HMS Endeavour and HMS Resolution charted Australia, New Zealand and Antarctica. He was the first person to circumnavigate the globe in both directions.

Scarborough Pudding

The first thing to say is do not be put off by tapioca! It cooks down completely to thicken the fruit juices.

85g/3oz tapioca, 55g/2oz sugar (or more, to taste), 570ml/1 pt water, 10g/4oz damsons (pricked with a fork) or red plums (stoned and cut up).

Put everything in a pan and bring to the boil, stirring to stop it sticking. Pour into a greased ovenproof dish, and put into an oven preheated to 170°C/325°F/gas mark 3. Bake for about an hour, stirring half way through. Serve warm or cold, with cream and sugar to taste. Serves 4.

Left: Robin Hoods Bay. Arthur Wainwright's Coast to Coast route traverses England from the Irish Sea coast at St Bees through the Yorkshire Dales, the Vale of Mowbray and the North York Moors to the North Sea at Robin Hoods Bay.

The Yorkshire Coast: Fishing and Holidays

Fishing was vitally important to the coastal towns and villages. At one time, Staithes was one of the largest fishing ports on the northeast coast of England, sending out fish three days a week by train. Whitby also has a long history of fishing, first herring and then whaling, and fish is still landed at the harbour. Fishing at Scarborough, Filey and Bridlington declined as they became popular tourist resorts.

Hull outgrew the other ports as it had a larger harbour that could take the bigger trawlers which were fishing further away. However, the fishing industry collapsed from the 1970s onwards, as a result of fishing restrictions and competition from other countries.

Scarborough's development as a holiday resort began in 1620 when spa water was discovered. However, it was the coming of the railways in the 1850s that turned it into a popular and busy resort. Anne Brontë of Haworth retired here, and on her death in 1849 was buried in St Mary's churchyard.

The Victorians built the first iron pier on the northeast coast at Saltburn by the Sea (above) and it is the last left standing. Saltburn also has the oldest water balanced cliff tramway in Britain, linking town and pier 40 metres below. The Cleveland Way follows a steep path up to Huntcliff, which was the site of a Roman Signal Station.

Above right: Bridlington harbour.

Below right: Winter sunrise at Filey. The Royal Crescent was the most fashionable address in the North of England for 100 years from 1850. In 1945 Butlin's Holiday camp opened near the town, complete with a railway station for the 10,000 holiday makers, but it closed in 1984 as the British increasingly took holidays abroad.

Spurn Head (above) extends 5½ km into the Humber estuary, but is only 50 metres wide in places. It is now a nature reserve, but has the man-made remains of disused lighthouses and wartime defences.

Withernsea's famous inland lighthouse (left) holds a museum and a tribute to the 1950s film star Kay Kendall.

The Humber Bridge (right) took eight years to build, and opened in 1981. The geology was unsuitable for a tunnel and a suspension bridge design was chosen as it does not need support piers which might obstruct the constantly moving navigable channel of the Humber.

Apple Fritters

225g/8oz plain flour, 85g/3oz caster sugar, 1 egg (beaten), 285ml/½pt milk, 7g/¼oz/1 tsp dried yeast, 110g/4oz grated apple, 85g/3oz currants, 85g/3oz raisins.

Warm the milk to the point where it feels very warm, but you can still comfortably hold your finger in it. Dissolve the yeast and a teaspoon of the sugar in the milk. Leave in a warm place for about 15 minutes, or until frothy.

Sieve the flour, make a well in the centre and drop in the egg. Start whisking the egg, bringing the flour in gradually. As it thickens, pour in the milk mixture in stages, to make a smooth batter. Stir in the fruit and the remaining sugar.

Cover the bowl with a tea towel and put in a warm place for at least a couple of hours, by which time the mixture should be bubbling well. Heat a frying pan with a film of oil on the bottom. Give the mixture a stir then drop about a tablespoon onto the pan. It should sizzle gently, then turn the heat right down so the sugar doesn't burn. Bubbles will rise to the surface and burst. The fritter is ready to turn over when the holes are staying open and the top surface no long looks liquid, which should take less than two minutes. Flip over and cook the other side for a minute. Makes about 20.

These fritters are the sweet cousins of crumpets and pikelets. The batter can be used in stages, as it will keep until the next day in a pantry or cool place. However one recipe suggests leaving it for three days until the fruit starts to ferment!

Flamborough Head (left) is one of the most spectacular lengths of chalk cliffs in Britain. It is one of the largest sites of nesting sea birds in England, and has a rare colony of gannets.

Hull's city centre (right) is a mixture of the old and the new around the restored dock areas.

Above: Hornsea Mere is the largest freshwater lake in Yorkshire, and is of glacial origin. It is popular with visitors and alive with wildlife as it is fringed with reedbeds, fen and carr.

Below: A view over the Vale of Pickering from Staxton Brow, with the dry pale yellow of summer grass and the blue haze of lavender.

Frumenty

Frumenty was an alternative to porridge made with wheat, and was popular in Yorkshire and the northeast. The wheat was slowly cooked in water for several hours, and then milk, salt, sugar and nutmeg were added before eating. In towns, the pre-cooked wheat was sold as 'creed wheat'.

In particular, the dish was served on Christmas Eve, when raisins, currants and sultanas were added, along with spices including nutmeg and cloves. This was then served with rum or brandy and followed by apple pie, cheese and cake.

Right: At one time there were over 200 windmills across The Wolds grinding the corn that made the area the 'bread basket' of Yorkshire. Skidby is the last remaining working windmill in Yorkshire. It is a four-sailed tower mill built in 1821 by Norman and Smithson of Hull. The adjacent warehouses are the home of the Museum of East Riding Rural Life.

Below: Bishop Burton is one of the most picturesque villages in the East Riding, with white painted buildings around two ponds.

The East Riding:
Minsters, Churches and Spires

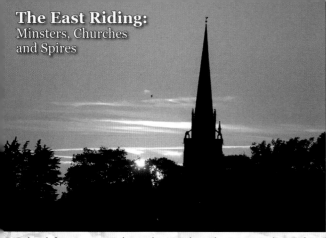

Left: Patrington church. The spire of the 13th century St Patrick's church can be seen for miles, and is known as the Queen of Holderness.

Below left: Hedon's church of St. Augustine was started around 1190, and is known as the King of Holderness.

Below right: Howden. The Prince-Bishops of Durham were given Howdenshire following the Norman Conquest. They created a palace and a grammar school and started to build the Minster Church. The Pilgrimage of Grace (1536) rebelled against the Dissolution of the Monasteries, and marched behind the cross of Howden Minster, a symbol of their faith which they feared would be seized. The church is still in use, but the rest is in ruins following the Dissolution.

York Ham

York ham has had a long reputation for quality, both in Britain and abroad. In part this was due to the local breed of Large White pig. The hams were probably produced across the county of Yorkshire, rather than just around York. In the past, food products were often named after the place they were shipped from, rather than where they were produced. Sometimes York ham is smoked, but there is no evidence for the legend that they were smoked over the sawdust produced by the building of York Minster.

Right: St Helen, Welton. One of the smaller and more picturesque churches of East Yorkshire.

Above: A monastery was founded in Beverley by John, bishop of York. When he died in 721 AD he was buried in a chapel of the Saxon church. The Minster was started in 1220 and was built around his tomb.

The present Minster is one of the finest Gothic churches in England, and contains elements of three styles: Early English, Decorated and Perpendicular. The facade of the west end of the Minster has many fine statutes. Siward was a Scandinavian Earl of Northumbria during the reign of King Cnut (1016-1035). At that time, Northumbria extended north from the Mersey and Humber to the Firth of Forth. In 1054 he led a campaign against the Scots, defeating Mac Bethad mac Findláich, the Macbeth of Shakespeare's play.

Mentioned in the Domesday book, Shambles (left) is Europe's best preserved Medieval street. Shambles were historically streets of butchers' houses and shops where livestock was slaughtered and sold, the word coming from the Anglo-Saxon 'sceamol'.

York was established by the Romans in 71 AD as Eboracum. It was the capital of the Anglian kingdom of Northumbria from 415 AD onwards, until it was taken by the Vikings in 866 AD and renamed Jórvík.

The medieval city walls originally included four main gates or 'bars', Bootham Bar, Monk Bar, Walmgate Bar and Micklegate Bar (left), and extended for about two miles. The walls were not just for defence as they were used to collect taxes from people passing into the city.

York Butter Biscuits

8oz/225g self-raising flour, 3oz/85g butter, 3oz/85g caster sugar, 5 tbs/75ml milk. Makes about 30.

Beat together butter and sugar until light and creamy. Beat in milk and flour gradually until it all comes together. Chill for an hour. Roll out about 3 mm thick, and cut 70 mm rounds.

Put on greased baking sheets, and bake for about 15 minutes at 170°C/325°F/ gas mark 3, until tinged light brown.

Above: York Minster. York's first Minster was built for the baptism of the Anglo-Saxon King Edwin of Northumbria on Easter Sunday in 627 AD. It was rebuilt in stone which survived the Viking period, the Normans replacing it with a substantial cathedral after the Conquest. During the 250 years following 1220, the cathedral was again rebuilt largely into the form it is today. The Great East Window is the world's largest single expanse of medieval stained glass.

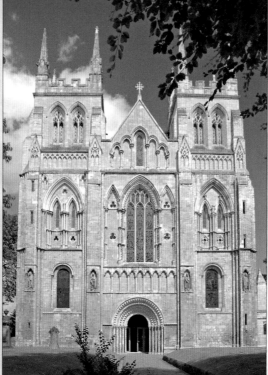

Left: Selby Abbey was founded in 1069 and became one of the wealthiest houses in Yorkshire. Following the dissolution of the monasteries the Church was left standing and became the Parish Church.

Despite fires and collapsed towers, it has survived as the only entire Benedictine Church in Yorkshire. It contains some outstanding stained glass windows, including the Jesse window which is second only in England to the West Window of York Minster.

Yorkshire Gingerbread

225g/8oz self raising flour, ½ tsp bicarbonate of soda, 1½ tsp ginger, 110g/4oz butter, 110g/4oz golden syrup, 110g/4oz dark soft brown sugar, 1 beaten egg, 5 tbs milk.

Grease and line an 18 cm/7" round cake tin. Gently melt butter, syrup and sugar together in a pan. Sift dry ingredients into a bowl, then beat in contents of pan. Beat in the egg and enough milk to make a thick batter.

Pour quickly into the tin and bake at 170°C/325°F/gas mark 3 for 50 minutes or until it is firm in the centre. Allow to cool in the tin, during which time it may sink in the centre. It improves with keeping for a few days before eating.

Above: Tadcaster's well water was ideal for brewing bitter beer, and Samuel Smith's Old Brewery is the oldest brewery in Yorkshire, established in 1758. They still ferment their beer in traditional Yorkshire slatestone 'squares', using a strain of yeast that originated in the 19th century. The dray horses used for delivery are stabled behind the Angel & White Horse in the right foreground and the brewery is the next building along. The chimney behind is part of John Smith's New Brewery, further up the road.

Above right: Wetherby used to be an important staging post for coach travellers between London and Edinburgh. It was also significant for its Statute Fair, which was held every November for the hiring of local servants. The Statute of Labours was introduced in the 14th century following the Black Death and many Yorkshire towns held fairs. However, the Industrial Revolution changed how labour was hired, and the fairs became centred on leisure and fun. The town is now best known for its racecourse.

Yorkshire Teacakes

500g/1 lb flour, 2 tsp sugar, 2 tsp instant dried yeast, 1 tsp salt, 45g/1½oz lard or butter, 150ml/¼ pt cold milk, 150ml/¼ pt boiling water.

Mix together the dry ingredients. Pour the water over the fat and allow it to melt, then mix in the milk. If the liquid is too hot to keep your finger in it comfortably, allow it to cool. Pour nearly all of the liquid onto the dry ingredients and starting bringing it together with your hands. The dough should form a soft and slightly sticky ball - add more liquid as needed. Knead for a few minutes, then cover with a damp cloth and leave to rise in a warm place until doubled in size - about an hour. Then, knead the dough lightly, divide into six and shape into flattened rounds. Place well apart on greased baking trays, cover with a damp cloth and leave to rise for another hour. Bake for about 15 minutes at 220°C/425°F/gas mark 7.

Yorkshire teacakes are the equivalent of Lancashire's balmcakes, or baps, buns or rolls in other parts of Britain. As such, they are usually plain, but many recipes give a sweet option; add about 125g/4oz of currants and double the sugar, then divide the dough into eight.

The Yorkshire of James Herriot

Above: Thirsk town centre.

Alf Wight wrote about his experiences of being a vet under the pseudonym of James Herriot. Writing mostly during the 1970s, his books were turned into two films and the BBC TV drama 'All Creatures Great and Small', which ran to ninety episodes from 1978 to 1990.

Right: Alf Wight's veterinary surgery was at 23 Kirkgate, Thirsk, the 'Skeldale House' in the books. It is now a museum which recreates a veterinary practice of the 1940s.

Much of the filming of the BBC TV series was done in the Yorkshire Dales. Arkengarthdale (left) featured in the opening sequences, and Askrigg was used for Darrowby. The building which featured as Skeldale House is opposite the church (below), and the nearby King's Arms became the Drover's Arms.

Yorkshire's sheep

Above left: Rough Fells are one of the largest mountain sheep in Britain and very hardy. They are mainly found in the western part of the Yorkshire Dales.

Below left: Teeswaters are also large sheep, but with a long fleece good for worsted suiting, knitting wools and wool blends. They are bred with upland breeds to get the best of both, the lambs being called Mashams. The fleece of this Masham lamb will reach the ground by the end of the winter.

Above: Swaledales originated as a breed just after the First World War when a group of farmers living near Tan Hill Inn, where Cumberland, Durham and Yorkshire meet, formed a Society. The Swaledale rapidly gained popularity through it's hardiness and mothering abilities, and is now one of the commonest hill breeds across Yorkshire and Cumbria.

Bottom right: At the centre of Masham, surrounded by Georgian houses, is the large market place. An annual sheep fair was held here of up to 80,000 head, including flocks from Fountains and Jervaulx Abbeys. The prosperity of Yorkshire Monasteries was built on sheep, cheese and wool.

Masham was allocated to the Minster of York in the medieval period, but due to its wealth and distance from York it was given a 'Peculiar' Court to run its own church affairs. This is the story behind the name of Theakston Brewery's famous Old Peculier Ale. Theakstons, founded in 1827, was joined in Masham by the Black Sheep Brewery in 1992.

YORKSHIRE PARKIN

225g/8oz self-raising flour, 225g/8oz oatmeal, 225g/8oz butter, 225g/8oz light soft brown sugar, 110g/4oz treacle, 110g/4oz golden syrup, 150ml/¼pt milk, 2 eggs, 4 tsp ginger.

Sieve together the dry ingredients. Melt the butter, sugar, treacle and syrup in a pan, then mix into the dry ingredients. Beat the eggs with the milk and beat into the mixture. Pour into a greased and lined 25x18cm/10"x7" tin. Bake for one hour at 170°C/325°F/gas mark 3; it will still be soft and may sink in the centre. Allow to cool in the tin. Keep a few days before eating, preferably a week. The oatmeal will soften and the flavours will develop and mature.

This is a modern example of parkin, which rises more and does not sink so much as it cools. A novel way of taking advantage of the 'sad' nature of parkin was handwritten in a recipe book from Carlisle, where the author suggested that the depression should be filled with rum!

PARKIN MOGGY THARF THOR AND VIKINGS

Some cakes have a long history. Tharf cake, from the Anglo-Saxon 'þeorf' or Old Norse 'þjarfr', was originally unleavened bread, made simply with oatmeal and butter, with honey added on special occasions. It was rolled flat and thin, and baked over a fire. The sweetened kind became associated with a series of Christian festivals in early November, including All Saints Day, All Souls' Day, All Hallows and Martinmas, which displaced the Celtic festival of Samain, the Feast of the Dead. A feature of Samain was bonfires - a tradition which was readily incorporated into Guy Fawkes Night after 1605.

Through the 19th century, treacle replaced honey and ginger, the cheapest of spices, was included. However, the bigger change followed the introduction of the domestic oven and baking powder. The mixture could then either be made wet and baked in a tin to rise into a cake, or made into a dough and rolled thin and baked as a biscuit. Along with this came a change of name, parkin for the cake and parkins for the biscuit. There is a traditional variation called moggy which contains flour only and has a reputation for being especially sticky. Once again it is thought that the name is derived from the Anglo-Saxon, 'múga', or Old Norse, 'múgi', a heap or mow of corn.

Recipes for parkin are tremendously variable in terms of ingredients and proportions, but with no consistent difference between different northern counties. The most significant variation is the proportion of wheatflour to oatmeal and whether it contains egg. Over time, parkin increasingly contained more flour and rising agent, so becoming lighter.

Cross in the church wall at Ellerburn (left) and carving at Kirkdale (right). Some Vikings settled in Ireland before coming to Britain, where their art picked up Celtic influences. This in turn interacted with the pre-existing Anglo-Saxon culture in Britain, especially after the Vikings converted to Christianity.

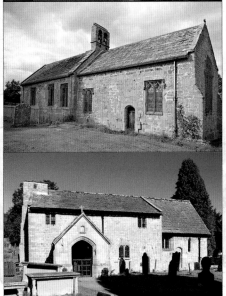

These three Anglo-Saxon churches, all have Anglo-Scandinavian features either near or built into them.

Top: St. Gregory's Minster, Kirkdale. Above the south door is a sundial with a dedication to Orm, son of Gamel, who had the church rebuilt between 1055 and 1065. Few places from this period can be dated so precisely.

Middle: St. Andrew, Finghall.

Bottom: St. Hilda, Ellerburn, which probably dates from around the same period as St. Gregory's as it is of similar design.

Yorkshire's Castles:
The Normans to the English Civil War

Below: There have been several fortifications on the headland at Scarborough including an Iron Age fort and a Roman lookout post. Later, the Viking 'Kormáks saga' refers to a castle being built at 'Skarðaborg'. The present castle is built round Henry II's 12th century keep. It was used as billets during the Jacobite invasion of 1745, was shelled by German cruisers in 1914 and had an important role during World War Two.

Above: Clifford's Tower, York. A timber fort on a motte was built by William the Conqueror in 1068 as a statement of power. It was burned down in 1190 in a massacre of the city's Jews. The fort was rebuilt in timber but collapsed in 1245 after which Henry III ordered it to be rebuilt in stone. This is the present building, which is about 15m high and 60m in diameter. Its design was unique in England, a 'quatrefoil' of four overlapping circles.

Below: Barden Tower in Wharfedale was the principal hunting lodge of the ancient Forest of Barden. It was extensively repaired in 1774.

Left: Helmsley Castle dates from around 1120. Most of the surviving stonework was built during the late 12th and 13th centuries by the crusader Robert de Roos and his descendants. The high, keep-like east tower is an unusual D-shaped in plan. It was only tested militarily once during the Civil War when it held out for three months under siege by the Parliamentarians in 1644.

Yorkshire Teabread

175g/6oz sultanas, 175g/6oz currants, 225ml/8 fl oz cold tea, 110g/4oz dark soft brown sugar, 1 egg (beaten), 225g/8oz self-raising flour.

Put the tea, dried fruit and sugar in a bowl, stir and leave overnight. The next day, beat the egg with the milk and stir into the mixture along with the flour, using a metal spoon. Pour into a greased and lined 22x11x6 cm/2 lb loaf tin. Bake for between an hour and 1¼ hours at 170°C/325°F/gas mark 3 or until cooked through. Turn out when cool.

The top may seem firm, but will soften by the next day. It keeps for about a week, and improves for the first few days of keeping.

Almond Cheesecakes

Filling: 85g/3oz ground almonds, 4 eggs, 170g/6oz caster sugar, grated rind of 3 lemons and juice of one, 110g/4oz butter.

Puff pastry: 180g/6½oz. Roll out the pastry and line 18 sections of two 12-hole bun trays.

Beat the eggs, then beat in the almonds, followed by the sugar and lemon. Gently heat the butter, and when just liquid, beat it into the mixture. Pour into a double boiler, or a metal or pyrex bowl placed in a pan of boiling water, and stirring constantly, heat until thickened. Share out the mixture between the pastry cases and bake at 220°C/425°F/gas mark 7 for about 10 minutes, or until the filling is browned and the pastry is cooked.

Cheesecakes, Yorkshire Curd Tart & Richmond Maids of Honour

Curd or cheese tarts have a long history, having first been recorded in Roman cookbooks. Although Curd Tarts are now a Yorkshire speciality, they were once part of a well known wider tradition across Britain and Europe. This is something Yorkshire kept, rather than being a locally unique invention.

There are endless variations of these tarts in Yorkshire, including different spices and other ingredients such as almonds or rice flour. Almonds were imported in large quantities to the Courts of Medieval England, and were a very common ingredient. While Richmond in Surrey lays claim to Maids of Honour through the accolade of Henry VIII (1491-1547), it is likely that Richard III's kitchens at Middleham were producing something similar 24 years earlier.

The almond cheesecake recipe above was contributed to a fundraising cookbook of the early 20th century and is a reminder of royal cooking in the Medieval period.

Bolton Castle, Wensleydale (above) was built by Sir Richard Le Scrope, Lord Chancellor of England. Mary Queen of Scots was imprisoned here in 1569 after she was captured on The Shawl, near Leyburn. Although no more than a fortified manor house, it held out for a few months for the Royalists during the Civil War.

Richmond castle (right) is one of the oldest stone castles in England, and was started in 1071. The tower remains to its full height, rising above some fine Georgian buildings around the large cobbled market place. The honour of Richmond was one of the three largest feudal holdings created by William the Conqueror. The connection with Richmond in Surrey is that after Henry VII (1457-1509) rebuilt the royal palace at Sheen on the Thames, he renamed it after the family title of Earl of Richmond.

Yorkshire's Castles: Kings, Barons & The House of York

Middleham Castle emerged as an important centre of government in the north of England by the end of the 12th century. Based on a hall-keep design, military effectiveness was combined with luxurious chambers to create a fortified palace by the mid-15th century. It was the childhood and favourite home of Richard III (1452-1485), the last King of the House of York and the last English king to die in battle, at Bosworth Field. The White Rose of the House of York is still the emblem of Yorkshire.

Yorkshire's Castles:
From Defence to Peace

Burton Agnes Hall (left) in East Yorkshire is one of the finest examples of Elizabethan domestic architecture in Britain. Nearby Sewerby Hall (above) has a history of reconstruction since the Viking Syward first had a farmstead here. The present facade is Georgian, dating from between 1714 and 1720.

Castle Howard was mostly built between 1699 and 1712 for the 3rd Earl of Carlisle, to a design by Sir John Vanbrugh. The word 'castle' continued to be used for English country houses after the period of fortified castle-building had ended. Castle Howard was used as 'Brideshead' in both Granada Television's 1981 adaption and the 2008 cinema version of Evelyn Waugh's novel 'Brideshead Revisited'.

Skipton Castle is intimately tied to the history of the Clifford family, who were granted the property and nearby land by Edward II in 1310. During the Civil War it was the last Royalist bastion in the North, holding out over a three-year siege, falling in 1645. It was 'slighted' after the Civil War, but the castle was skillfully restored by Lady Anne Clifford, a remarkable woman who also restored many of the family properties in Westmorland and Cumberland.

Yorkshire Mint Pasty

Shortcrust pastry: 180g/6oz flour, 90g/3oz butter or half and half butter and lard.

Filling: 180g/6oz currants, 60g/2oz light soft brown sugar, 45g/1½oz butter (softened), 7tbs chopped fresh mint, some chopped mixed peel if liked.

Makes eight pasties.

Make up the pastry as described on the inside back page. Roll out, and use a saucer to cut out eight circles. Blend the filling together then share it out, placing equal amounts to one side of each circle. Moisten the edge of the pastry, fold over and seal. Brush with milk and sprinkle with demerara sugar if liked. Bake at 190°C/375°F/gas mark 5 for 25-30 minutes or until the pastry is browned.

There are many varieties of rich dried fruit pastries across Britain, but the addition of mint is unique to Yorkshire. The earliest record is in an early 19th century reference.

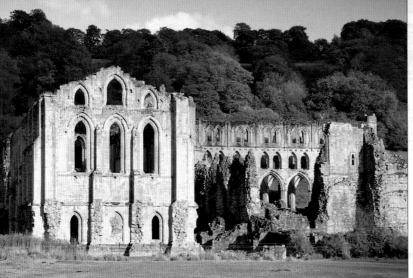

Founded in 1132, Rievaulx Abbey (above left) was the first Cistercian outpost for the reform and colonisation of northern England and Scotland. By the middle of the 13th century, it was one of the richest Abbeys in England. The Black Death of 1348-9 was devastating for all the monasteries, but more so for Rievaulx as the number of members fell from around 700 to eighteen. In the late 15th century dairy farming replaced sheep farming.

A dispute at St. Mary's Abbey in York in 1132 led to the founding of Fountains Abbey (below left) by thirteen monks. Thurstan, Archbishop of York gave them a site where they could found a new, more devout monastery. Within three years it was admitted to the Cistercian Order.

Whitby Abbey (below right) was founded in 657 AD by King Oswy of Northumbria following his unexpected victory over Penda, the pagan king of Mercia, two years earlier. St Hilda established its success, and its importance was recognised when it hosted the synod of 664 AD. This resolved the religious differences in Britain between the Ionian and Roman traditions in favour of Rome. The Abbey was destroyed by the Vikings in 867-9 AD and was re-established in 1078.

The long stairway to the ruined Abbey provided inspiration for Bram Stoker's Dracula.

Yorkshire's Abbeys & Monasteries

By the end of the Medieval period, Yorkshire had around seventy monasteries, more than any other areas of the country. By the middle of the 13th century Fountains and Rievaulx were two of England's richest religious houses.

Byland (above) was the third great Yorkshire Cistercian abbey, which held over 200 monks and lay brothers at its peak. The outstanding feature is the circular rose window which was probably used as the model for York Minster.

The Cistercian system of lay brothers was essential to the growth of the monasteries. They took the routine jobs, most importantly looking after the vast flocks of sheep, which gave the monks more time for religious observance. The monks were committed to long silences, a subsistence diet and a habit of coarse undyed sheep's wool without underwear, from which they became known as 'White Monks'.

Yorkshire's Abbeys & Monasteries

Left: Bolton Priory. The land at Bolton was granted to the Augustinians in 1154 by Lady Alice de Rumilly. The majority of the building was constructed by 1220, but there are some later additions, including the 14th century gateway and the 16th century west tower. After the Dissolution of the Monasteries much of the priory was dismantled, but the original nave was incorporated into the present Priory church.

Below: Jervaulx Abbey was founded in 1156, as a daughter house of Byland Abbey. At its peak, the abbey owned half of the valley and was famed for horse breeding, a tradition which continues today around Middleham. It was also the original home of Wensleydale cheese. Jervaulx is open to the public, and is maintained as an enchanting, charming and atmospheric ruin by its private owners with wild flowers and plants freely exploring its many nooks and crannies.

Yorkshire Scones

180g/6oz self-raising flour, 30g/1oz caster sugar, 60g/2oz butter, 1 egg, milk to mix.

Stir sugar into flour, then rub in butter. Mix in egg and enough milk to make a soft, but not sticky, dough. Roll out into one round, 25mm/1" thick. Make shallow cuts across top to mark out wedges, and bake at 220°C/425°F/gas mark 7 for 12-15 minutes, until risen and lightly browned.

Yorkshire scones are made in one large round rather than several small ones.

Gisborough Priory (right) was an Augustinian priory founded by ancestors of the Bruce family, later Kings of Scotland. The skeleton of the east end of the 14th century church dominates the ruins.

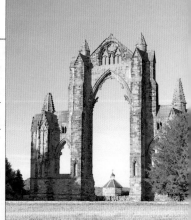

Yorkshire Curd Tart

225g/8oz curd cheese, 60g/2oz sugar, 1 tbs cream or 30g/1oz butter, 90g/3oz currants, 2 beaten eggs, a little nutmeg or lemon rind, 1 tbs brandy (optional). Shortcrust pastry: 90g/3oz flour and 45g/1½oz butter.

Make up the pastry as described on the inside back page, and bottom line a 20cm/8" pie dish. Blend the cream or butter with the sugar, then beat in the cheese thoroughly. Mix in the other ingredients, and spoon into the pastry case.

Bake at 180°C/350°F/gas mark 4 for about 30 minutes, or until set and lightly browned.

To make small tarts: Line tartlet trays with the pastry and share out the filling. Bake for about 20 minutes.

Curd cheese can be made easily. Bring 2 litres/3.5 pints of full-fat milk (not long-life) almost to the boil. Turn off the heat and stir in the juice of two lemons. Stir gently until curdled, then drain off the whey through a sieve or muslin. This makes about 350g/12oz of curd cheese using homogenised full-fat milk. Semi-skimmed milk will produce less curds and creamy milk more. This curdling process is the first step in making any cheese.

Old recipes also used rennet or epsom salts to curdle the milk, but lemons are more convenient if curds are not being made often.

The whey can be used in recipes which ask for buttermilk, such as scones and soda bread. Any curds that are left over can be mixed with a little salt and eaten as it is or used in cooking.

Above: The Millennium sundial in Castleton, in Eskdale in the North York Moors, marks the village's former importance as a market town and local cheese production. It also marks where John Wesley preached in 1772.

Yorkshire Cheeses

From left to right: White Wensleydale and Blue Wensleydale from the Hawes Creamery, Mrs Bells Blue ewe's milk cheese from the Shepherds Purse Creamery in Thirsk, and the Swaledale Cheese Company's ewe's milk cheese. There is a strong Yorkshire tradition of eating cheese with fruit cake, and also apple pie.

Production of cheeses used to be widespread through Yorkshire. In Yarm, on the Yorkshire side of the River Tees near to Stockton-on-Tees, quarterly fairs were held. The second day of the October Fair was reserved for the sale of sheep and cheese, and in the early 1800s, between 300 and 400 wagon loads of cheese were brought to market.

Today Wensleydale cheese is probably the only Yorkshire cheese that most people could name. The monks of Jervaulx are credited with bringing the skills of making a blue, ewe's milk cheese from France to Yorkshire. The lay brothers took the cheesemaking skills they had learned from the monks into their farmhouses after the Dissolution of the Monasteries. Over time, cows milk gradually replaced ewes milk. Wensleydale cheese was traditionally made in the summer months, bluing naturally through the maturation process. However, during the 20th century, factory production led to the cheese being produced all year round and sold when young and still white.

Production flourished until the 1930s, but declined firstly as the Milk Marketing Board started offering guaranteed prices for milk, and then due to the restrictions of the Ministry of Food during World War II. The Hawes dairy might have closed in the 1930s but for Kit Calvert and the formation of the Wensleydale Cheesemakers Association. The Hawes Creamery was again saved in 1992 for Wensleydale cheese production. However the start of artisan cheesemaking from the 1980s revived a variety of traditional cheeses.

The story of Wensleydale cheese is common to other Yorkshire cheeses, many of which were lost However, cheesemaking has been revived in some of the Dales, along with the old names, including Cotherstone, Coverdale, Cleveland, Swaledale and Ribblesdale.

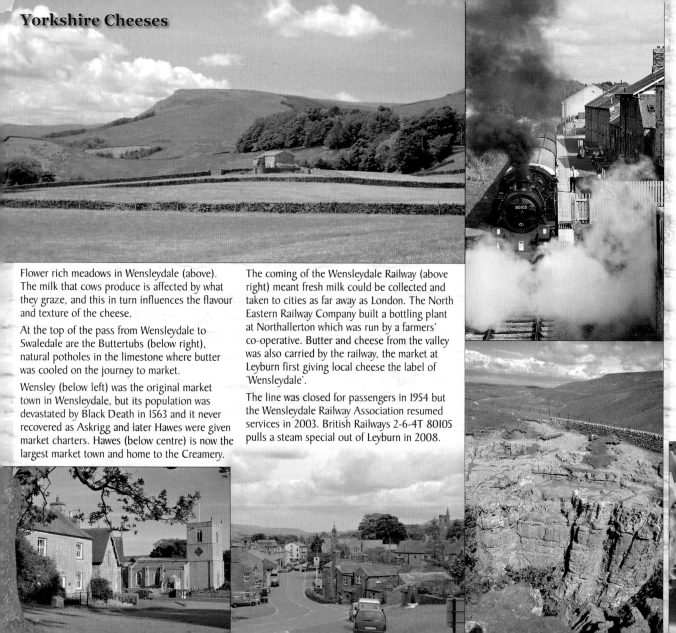

Yorkshire Cheeses

Flower rich meadows in Wensleydale (above). The milk that cows produce is affected by what they graze, and this in turn influences the flavour and texture of the cheese.

At the top of the pass from Wensleydale to Swaledale are the Buttertubs (below right), natural potholes in the limestone where butter was cooled on the journey to market.

Wensley (below left) was the original market town in Wensleydale, but its population was devastated by Black Death in 1563 and it never recovered as Askrigg and later Hawes were given market charters. Hawes (below centre) is now the largest market town and home to the Creamery.

The coming of the Wensleydale Railway (above right) meant fresh milk could be collected and taken to cities as far away as London. The North Eastern Railway Company built a bottling plant at Northallerton which was run by a farmers' co-operative. Butter and cheese from the valley was also carried by the railway, the market at Leyburn first giving local cheese the label of 'Wensleydale'.

The line was closed for passengers in 1954 but the Wensleydale Railway Association resumed services in 2003. British Railways 2-6-4T 80105 pulls a steam special out of Leyburn in 2008.

Yorkshire Fruit Cakes

180g/6oz plain flour, 180g/6oz caste sugar, 120g/4oz butter, 90g/3oz raisins, 90g/3oz currants, 30g/1oz glacé cherries (quartered), 30g/1oz ground almonds, 2 eggs (beaten), 1 tsp baking powder.

Cream the butter and sugar, then add the eggs slowly. This can be done with a wooden spoon or in a food processor. Stir in the fruit with a metal spoon, then sieve together the flour and baking powder and stir into the mix. Share out the mixture between nine muffin cases and bake at 180°C/350°F/gas mark 4 for 25 minutes, or until lightly browned and cooked through in the centre.

Traditionally fruit cakes are baked in large tins, which requires a cooking time of 2 hours or so. They are then stored before eating, as the flavour improves and they become moister. However, they are also delicious baked like this, some eaten fresh from the oven and the rest kept. This recipe is based on a fruit slab recipe from 50 years ago.

West Riding Pudding

Shortcrust pastry: 80g/3oz flour, 40g/1½oz butter (cold).
Filling: 2 eggs (beaten), 110g/4oz butter (softened), 110g/4oz self-raising flour, 110g/4oz caster sugar, flavouring of either ½ tsp vanilla essence, or the grated rind of half a lemon or a few drops of almond essence. 110g/4oz raspberry or strawberry conserve. Serves 4.

Make up the pastry as described on the inside back page.

Make the filling by creaming the butter and sugar together. Add the flavouring, and beat in the eggs and the flour in stages. This can be done by hand or in a food processor.

Line the bottom of a 20 cm/8" pie or flan dish with pastry. Spread the conserve over the pastry, then put the cake mixture over the top. Bake at 180°C/350°F/gas mark 4 for about 50 minutes or until cooked through in the centre. Serve warm with custard sauce.

West Riding Pudding is a classic pudding and several places in Britain have claimed it with their name.

Pennine Yorkshire:
Haworth and the Brontës

Haworth is an attractive town with stone buildings and a cobbled street rising up the hill (below), but its fame is based on its connection with the Brontë sisters. The family was brought up in the Parsonage, which is now a museum (above).

John Wesley was a frequent visitor to Haworth, where he gave all day sermons. The evangelical zeal of Wesley and his followers, including William Grimshaw, a parson at the Parish Church, earned them the name of 'Methodists'. They only separated from the Church of England after Wesley's death in 1795, after which Methodist congregations started to build the chapels found in many Dales villages.

Below: The Keighley & Worth Valley Railway was closed by Beeching in 1962, but reopened just six years later. It has been used as filming location for both cinema and TV, most famously for the original 1970 version of 'The Railway Children'. This former LMS 'Jinty' 0-6-0 tank engine is similar to the engines that regularly worked the branch in the 1930s.

Hebden Bridge (above) developed in the valley next to the older settlement of Heptonstall. The weaving of wool was an important home-based occupation in Heptonstall, and the rows of weavers' cottages were built with long windows on the top floor to provide light for the hand-looms. However, power looms took over in the 19th century, and factory mills were built in Hebden Bridge where they could take power from the rivers. Hebden Bridge also had an important place in the history of the co-operative movement, in common with many towns on the Lancashire-Yorkshire border.

Yorkshire's 'Rhubarb Triangle'

Rhubarb was brought to Britain from Siberia and thrives in the cool, wet northern climate. No northern kitchen garden or allotment is complete without some rhubarb crowns.

The earliest rhubarb of the season is from crowns which are 'forced' in the dark. Gardeners will cover the crowns with tubs in late winter to get the early long pink tender stalks. However, in the 'Rhubarb Triangle', roughly between Leeds, Wakefield and Bradford, commercial producers built large light-proof sheds, and Yorkshire became a centre of rhubarb production. Keeping light out is so important that the stalks were picked by candlelight, and still are to this day. 'Yorkshire Forced Rhubarb' Is a protected name by Europe for production in this area.

Rhubarb Crumble

The robust flavour of an oat based crumble goes very well against the tartness of rhubarb.

Filling:
450g/1 lb rhubarb, 90g/3oz granulated sugar, 1 tbs plain flour

Cut the rhubarb into pieces about 20 mm long, and put in a greased ovenproof dish. Mix the flour and sugar, and stir in with the rhubarb.

Crumble: 120g/4oz porridge oats, 120g/4oz plain wholemeal flour, 90g/3oz butter, 60g/2oz light soft brown sugar, 30g/1oz stem ginger preserved in syrup, drained.

Mix the oats and flour, then rub in the butter until the mixture resembles breadcrumbs. Chop the ginger and stir it into the mixture along with sugar. Spread the crumble over the rhubarb and bake at 180°C/350°F/gas mark 4 for 40 minutes.

Where the recipes come from...

The recipes in this booklet have been collected, compared, combined and retested from an extensive collection of recipe books. The most useful are the contributions that were made to community recipe books such as those shown here. In the older cookbooks, the recipes are organised by the place they had in the menu, and with big sections for cakes and sweets. In the later ones there is an awareness of 'traditional recipes' which are placed in a separate section. The most useful cookbooks are usually the earlier ones, up to around 1960.

These recipe books are an interesting form of literature. They were produced within a locality by a community group, often a church or the Women's Institute, usually to raise funds for a project. The books were published by small local printers in short runs. Normally the contributors were women, and the recipes reveal issues around how food was viewed, as well as wealth and class and geography, The largest sections are usually for cakes, biscuits and pastries, which were the types of food where girls were encouraged to show off their cooking ability. It also reflected the kind of food that was regarded as 'appropriate' for women - sweet and dainty. This idea was established by the domestic science movement in the 19th century and was promoted through cookery publishing from Mrs Beeton onwards.

The community recipe book was one of the few outlets for women's writing in the 19th and early 20th century. The other form of writing often associated with women, biography, shares some features with the recipe books, in particular the connection with self, family and relationships. However the community recipe book is an almost unique form of communal self-expression, and they represent a sharing of a common wealth of knowledge.

Sadly these books are too often regarded as trivial ephemera, and thrown away. Ironically, the ones which were most used, splashed and stained with the pages annotated with cook's notes, are the ones least likely to survive. But within those that do, there are not just the names of the contributors, but also a record of their social life and the foods that they made within their lifetimes.